Love Sonnets

Love Sonnets

SELECTED AND WITH NOTES BY
LOUIS UNTERMEYER

ILLUSTRATED BY BEN SHAHN

Harmony books

A DIVISION OF CROWN PUBLISHERS

NEW YORK

ACKNOWLEDGMENTS

The translation of Heine's "To My Mother" is copyright, 1937, by Louis Untermeyer and reprinted with his permission. "Renouncement" by Alice Meynell is reprinted with the permission of Sir Francis Meynell.

ISBN Number: 0-517-51313-7 (cloth edition)

Library of Congress Card Catalog Number: 73-85859

Printed in Italy by Arnoldo Mondadori Editore, Sp A

Introduction

The word "sonnet" is derived from the Italian "sonetto," literally "a little sound," suggestively a short strain of verbal melody. This explains the sonnet's brevity as well as its place of origin; it was cultivated in Italy as early as the thirteenth century. Petrarch, in the fourteenth century, established it with such skill that, although many variants have become popular, the pure Petrarchan (or Italian) sonnet is still the favorite form. It is a poem whose subject is almost always a treatment of love. Its structure is precise. The Petrarchan sonnet consists of fourteen lines, each line with five stresses (or beats) and all the lines rhymed. The first eight lines (the octave) are separated from the remaining six lines (the sestet). The rhyme scheme of the octave is *a-b-b-a-a-b-b-a;* that of the sestet is either *c-d-c-d-c-d* or *c-d-e-c-d-e.*

For a long time the Petrarchan sonnet was the norm. Then poets, resenting the rule that separated the sonnet into octave and sestet, united the two parts. They also began to vary the arrangement of the rhymes. The Shakespearian (or Elizabethan) sonnet is composed of three four-line stanzas (quatrains) and a concluding couplet with this order of rhymes: *a-b-a-b, c-d-c-d, e-f-e-f, g, g.* The Spenserian sonnet tied the octave and sestet together by threading the rhymes throughout except for a separate rhyming couplet, such as: *a-b-a-b-b-c-b-c-c-d-c-d-e-e.* There have been so many departures from the originally strict rules that more than a dozen variations

could be classified. However, there is one thing which characterizes the sonnet and makes it immediately recognizable: classic or contemporary, it consists of fourteen lines. Those fourteen lines have been put to countless uses and have embodied innumerable themes. The sonnet's concision has compelled the poet to express himself with the greatest economy of words; the very tightness of its form has resulted in extraordinary compactness of thought and image.

In spite of its severe limitation, it is capable of the widest possible range of emotions: the beauty of life and the terror of death; elegiac sorrow and leaping joy; meditative questioning and the rapt acceptance of love. It is to the varied manifestations of love—delightful and desperate, filial and paternal, restrained and ecstatic—that this book is devoted.

Louis Untermeyer

For certain he hath seen all perfectness
    Who among other ladies hath seen mine:
    They that go with her humbly should combine
To thank their God for such peculiar grace.
So perfect is the beauty of her face
    That it begets in no wise any sign
    Of envy, but draws round her a clear line
Of love, and blessed faith, and gentleness.
Merely the sight of her makes all things bow:
    Not she herself alone is holier
    Than all; but hers, through her, are raised above.
From all her acts such lovely graces flow
    That truly one may never think of her
    Without a passion of exceeding love.

DANTE ALIGHIERI
Translated by
DANTE GABRIEL
ROSSETTI

9

Set me whereas the sun doth parch the green,
　Or where his beams do not dissolve the ice:
　In temperate heat, where he is felt and seen;
　In presence prest of people mad or wise;
Set me in high, or yet in low degree;
　In longest night or in the shortest day;
　In clearest sky, or where clouds thickest be;
　In lusty youth, or when my hairs are gray.
Set me in heaven, in earth, or else in hell,
　In hill or dale, or in the foaming flood;
　Thrall, or at large, alive whereso I dwell,
Sick or in health, in evil fame or good,
　Hers will I be; and only with this thought
Content myself although my chance be nought.

FRANCESCO PETRARCA
Translated by
HENRY HOWARD,
Earl of Surrey　**11**

I send you here a wreath of blossoms blown,
    And woven flowers at sunset gathered,
    Another dawn had seen them ruined, and shed
Loose leaves upon the grass at random strown.
By this, their sure example, be it known,
    That all your beauties, now in perfect flower,
    Shall fade as these, and wither in an hour,
Flowerlike, and brief of days, as the flower sown.

Ah, time is flying, lady—time is flying;
    Nay, 'tis not time that flies but we that go,
Who in short space shall be in churchyard lying,
    And of our loving parley none shall know,
Nor any man consider what we were.
Be therefore kind, my love, whilst thou art fair.

PIERRE DE RONSARD
Translated by
ANDREW LANG

13

More than most fair, full of the living fire
Kindled above unto the Maker near:
No eyes, but joys, in which all powers conspire,
That to the world naught else be counted dear:
Through your bright beams doth not the blinded guest
Shoot out his darts to base affection's wound,
But angels come, to lead frail minds to rest
In chaste desires, on heavenly beauty bound.
You frame my thoughts, and fashion me within,
You stop my tongue, and teach my heart to speak,
You calm the storm that passion did begin,
Strong through your cause, but by your virtue weak.
   Dark is the world where your light shined never,
   Well is he born that may behold you ever.

EDMUND SPENSER

15

My true love hath my heart and I have his,
By just exchange one for the other given.
I hold his dear, and mine he cannot miss,
There never was a better bargain driven.
His heart in me keeps me and him in one;
My heart in him his thoughts and senses guides.
He loves my heart, for once it was his own;
I cherish his, because in me it bides.
His heart his wound received from my sight;
My heart was wounded with his wounded heart,
For as from me on him his hurt did light
So still methought in me his hurt did smart.
Both equal hurt, in this change sought our bliss:
My true love hath my heart and I have his.

SIR PHILIP SIDNEY

17

Ah, were she pitiful as she is fair,
Or but as mild as she is seeming so,
Then were my hopes greater than my despair,
Then all the world were heaven, nothing woe.
Ah, were her heart relenting as her hand,
That seems to melt even with the mildest touch,
Then knew I where to seat me in a land
Under wide heavens, but yet there is none such.
So, as she shows, she seems the budding rose,
Yet sweeter far than is an earthly flower;
Sovran of beauty! like the spray she grows,
Compassed she is with thorns and cankered bower.
Yet were she willing to be plucked and worn
She would be gathered though she grew on thorn.

ROBERT GREENE

19

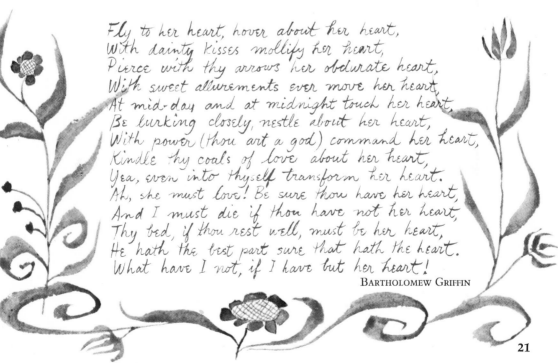

Fly to her heart, hover about her heart,
With dainty kisses mollify her heart,
Pierce with thy arrows her obdurate heart,
With sweet allurements ever move her heart,
At mid-day and at midnight touch her heart,
Be lurking closely, nestle about her heart,
With power (thou art a god) command her heart,
Kindle thy coals of love about her heart,
Yea, even into thyself transform her heart.
Ah, she must love! Be sure thou have her heart,
And I must die if thou have not her heart,
Thy bed, if thou rest well, must be her heart,
He hath the best part sure that hath the heart.
What have I not, if I have but her heart!

BARTHOLOMEW GRIFFIN

21

When men shall find thy flower, thy glory, pass,
And thou, with careful brow sitting alone,
Received hast this message from thy glass,
That tells the truth and says that all is gone;
Fresh shalt thou see in me the wounds thou madest,
Though spent thy flame, in me the heat remaining;
I that have loved thee thus before thou fadest,
My faith shall wax when thou art in thy waning.

The world shall find this miracle in me,
That fire can burn when all the matter's spent;
Then what my faith hath been, thyself shall see,
And that thou wast unkind, thou mayst repent.
Thou mayst repent that thou hast scorned my tears,
When winter snows upon thy sable hairs.

SAMUEL DANIEL

23

Since there's no help, come let us kiss and part;
Nay, I have done, you get no more of me;
And I am glad, yea, glad with all my heart
That thus so cleanly I myself can free.
Shake hands for ever, cancel all our vows,
And, when we meet at any time again,
Be it not seen in either of our brows
That we one jot of former love retain.

Now at the last gasp of Love's latest breath,
When, his pulse failing, Passion speechless lies,
When Faith is kneeling by his bed of death,
And Innocence is closing up his eyes—
Now if thou wouldst, when all have given him over,
From death to life thou might'st him yet recover.

MICHAEL DRAYTON

25

Shall I compare thee to a summer's day?
Thou art more lovely and more temperate.
Rough winds do shake the darling buds of May,
And summer's lease hath all too short a date:
Sometimes too hot the eye of heaven shines,
And often is his gold complexion dimmed:
And every fair from fair sometime declines,
By chance, or nature's changing course, untrimmed:
But thy eternal summer shall not fade
Nor lose possession of that fair thou owest;
Nor shall Death brag thou wanderest in his shade
When in eternal lines to time thou growest.
So long as men can breath, or eyes can see
So long lives this, and this gives life to thee.

WILLIAM SHAKESPEARE

27

It is a beauteous evening, calm and free;
The holy time is quiet as a nun
Breathless with adoration; the broad sun
Is sinking down in its tranquillity;
The gentleness of heaven broods o'er the sea:
Listen! the mighty Being is awake,
And doth with his eternal motion make
A sound like thunder—everlastingly.
Dear child! dear girl! that walkest with me here,
If thou appear untouched by solemn thought,
Thy nature is not therefore less divine:
Thou liest in Abraham's bosom all the year,
And worship'st at the Temple's inner shrine,
God being with thee when we know it not.

WILLIAM WORDSWORTH

29

I cry your mercy – pity – love! – aye, love!
 Merciful love that tantalizes not.
One-thoughted, never-wandering, guileless love,
 Unmasked, and being seen – without a blot!
O! let me have thee whole, – all – all – be mine!
 That shape, that fairness, that sweet minor zest
Of love, your kiss, – those hands, those eyes divine,
 That warm, white, lucent, million-pleasured breast,
Yourself – your soul – in pity give me all,
 Withhold no atom's atom or I die,
Or living on perhaps, your wretched thrall,
 Forget, in the mist of idle misery,
Life's purposes, – the palate of my mind
Losing its gust, and my ambition blind!

JOHN KEATS

31

Stubborn and proud, I carry my head high;
Haughty by birth, inflexible by mood,
I would not bow to any king; I would
Not even veil my candid gaze, not I.
But, mother, never let me dare deny
How soon my pride, my boastful hardihood
Shamed by your presence and solicitude,
Leaves me without one small departing sigh.

Is it your spirit that o'ermasters me,
Your lofty, penetrating soul that clears
The earth and cleaves to heaven, flying free.
Memory burns and rankles, for I know
How often I have brought your heart to tears,
The soft and suffering heart that loved me so.

HEINRICH HEINE
Translated by
LOUIS UNTERMEYER

How do I love thee? Let me count the ways.
I love thee to the depth and breadth and height
My soul can reach, when feeling out of sight
For the ends of Being and ideal Grace.
I love thee to the level of every day's
Most quiet need, by sun and candle-light.
I love thee freely, as men strive for right;
I love thee purely, as they turn from praise.
I love thee with the passion put to use
In my old griefs, and with my childhood's faith.
I love thee with a love I seemed to lose
With my lost saints – I love thee with the breath,
Smiles, tears, of all my life! – and, if God choose,
I shall but love thee better after death.

ELIZABETH BARRETT BROWNING

35

Your hands lie open in the long fresh grass,
The finger-points look through like rosy blooms;
Your eyes smile peace. The pasture gleams and glooms
'Neath billowing skies that scatter and amass.
All round our nest, far as the eye can pass,
Are golden kingcup-fields with silver edge
Where the cow-parsley skirts the hawthorn-hedge.
'Tis visible silence, still as the hour-glass.

Deep in the sun-searched growths the dragon-fly
Hangs like a blue thread loosened from the sky:
So this winged hour is dropt to us from above.
Oh! clasp we to our hearts, for deathless dower,
This close-companioned inarticulate hour
When twofold silence was the song of love.

DANTE GABRIEL ROSSETTI

Remember me when I am gone away,
Gone far away into the silent land;
When you can no more hold me by the hand,
Nor I half turn to go, yet turning stay.
Remember me when no more, day by day,
You tell me of our future that you planned;
Only remember me; you understand
It will be late to counsel then or pray.

Yet if you should forget me for a while
And afterwards remember, do not grieve;
For if the darkness and corruption leave
A vestige of the thoughts that once I had,
Better by far you should forget and smile
Than that you should remember and be sad.

CHRISTINA ROSSETTI

39

I must not think of thee; and, tired yet strong,
　　I shun the thought that lurks in all delight—
　　The thought of thee—and in the blue Heaven's height,
And in the sweetest passage of a song.
O just beyond the fairest thoughts that throng
　　This breast, the thought of thee waits hidden yet bright;
　　But it must never, never come in sight;
I must stop short of thee the whole day long.

But when sleep comes to close each difficult day,
　　When night gives pause to the long watch I keep,
　　And all my bonds I needs must loose apart,
Must doff my will as raiment laid away.
　　With the first dream that comes with the first sleep
　　I run, I run, I am gathered to thy heart.

ALICE MEYNELL

41

Notes on the Poems and Poets

DANTE ALIGHIERI (1265–1321) Dante (short for Durante) Alighieri was born in Florence and died in exile in Ravenna at fifty-six. Before he wrote the hundred cantos of his epical *Divine Comedy,* he had composed the *New Life,* which celebrated his love for Beatrice, whom he met when both were children. She died at twenty-four but remained his life-long inspiration. It is Beatrice who, in the *Divine Comedy,* acts as the poet's guide through Paradise.

FRANCESCO PETRARCA (1304–1374) What Beatrice was to Dante, Laura was to Petrarch. Scholar, poet, and patriot, Petrarch was one of the great figures of the Italian Renaissance. In his early twenties he saw Laura for the first time; who she may have been has never been authenticated. Petrarch made her a spiritual ideal, the unattainable mistress, the heroine of courtly love. The sonnets in her memory are perfect expressions of purified passion.

PIERRE DE RONSARD (1524–1585) Hailed by his generation as "prince of poets," Pierre de Ronsard was the dark star in France's sixteenth-century group known as the Pléiade—"dark" because of his belated discovery as well as because of his deafness. Influenced by his predecessors, especially Petrarch, Ronsard excelled in occasional, graceful, and lightly amatory verse.

EDMUND SPENSER (1552?–1599) Although Edmund Spenser is best known for the long and difficult allegory, *The Faerie Queene,* he is far more winning in his shorter poems. The eighty-eight sonnets in the sequence called *Amoretti* are as pure in thought as they are rich in images. They were inspired by Elizabeth Boyle, who became Spenser's wife and who shared his spectacular career from riches to rags.

SIR PHILIP SIDNEY (1554–1586) Sir Philip Sidney was one of the group that included Edmund Spenser; he echoed his friend's *Amoretti* with a sonnet sequence of his own: *Astrophel and Stella.* Reared in luxury, richly endowed, a favourite at court, appointed governor of a province when he was only thirty, he was, to borrow Chaucer's words, "a verray, parfit, gentil knight." Fatally wounded in battle, he passed his half-empty canteen to a dying soldier, saying, "Thy necessity is greater than mine."

ROBERT GREENE (1558?–1592) The Elizabethan era was a period of pomp, pageantry, and swashbuckling drama. One of its most notorious swaggerers was Robert Greene, whose red beard was a beacon of terror and whose boast was that he took as much delight in villainy as others did in godliness. Although well-born, he spent his days and nights carousing with coarse companions and died in miserable poverty. Somehow he managed to write a few exquisite lyrics and sonnets, and it is thought that Shakespeare was indebted to Greene for part of *King Henry the Sixth*.

BARTHOLOMEW GRIFFIN (1560?–1602) An obscure figure, whose birth date is a conjecture and whose career is uncertain, Bartholomew Griffin was the author of a sonnet sequence, *Fidessa, More Chaste Than Kind;* the third sonnet of the sequence, printed in an Elizabethan miscellany, *The Passionate Pilgrim,* was credited to Shakespeare. Besides being a poignant poem, "Her Heart" is a curiosity among sonnets, a tour de force with one word repeated fourteen times instead of the customary variation of rhymes.

SAMUEL DANIEL (1562–1619) Another popular set of sonnets with a single theme, *Delia,* was composed by Samuel Daniel. Spenser hailed the author as the "new shepherd late upsprung," and more than two hundred years later, Coleridge declared that Daniel's style was "such as any pure and manly writer of the present day—Wordsworth, for example—would use." Slight as it is, *Delia* has been ransacked by the anthologists for its picturesque and sometimes impassioned poems.

MICHAEL DRAYTON (1563–1631) Although it lacks the scope of Shakespeare's sonnets, Michael Drayton's sonnet sequence *Ideas Mirrour* suggests the range and richness that only Shakespeare could achieve. It breaks through the conventions of the form into a desire and desperation that sets it above most of the conventions of the period. Few sonnets have attained the sense of intensity—a mingling of hurt, bitterness, and hope—accomplished in the fourteen packed lines of "Since there's no help, come let us kiss and part."

WILLIAM SHAKESPEARE (1564–1616) William Shakespeare's one hundred and fifty-two collected sonnets have provoked countless speculations and endless controversies. Although they embody a story, the plot is vague and the development obscured by the order in which the sonnets appear. It is generally accepted that the sonnets are autobiographical and that they concern three individuals: the poet, a dear friend, and an ambiguous woman who is the mistress of both, a "dark lady" utterly unlike Petrarch's Laura and Dante's Beatrice. In Shakespeare's sequence the friend and the mistress become the twin objects of a complicated love that triumphs over time.

WILLIAM WORDSWORTH (1770–1850) Fifty years before William Wordsworth became poet laureate, he spent a year in Europe. He was twenty-two; he championed the French revolutionary party and fell in love with Annette Vallon, by whom he had a daughter, Carolyn. Returning to England, he turned from romance to reality, married his sister's friend, and grew increasingly conservative. In his thirties he revisited France and, with his ten-year-old daughter, took evening walks along the seashore. After one of those walks he composed a sonnet famous for the quality which Wordsworth praised as poetry in the Preface to the *Lyrical Ballads:* "the spontaneous overflow of powerful feelings" which "takes its origin from emotion recollected in tranquility."

JOHN KEATS (1795–1821) Except for his letters, nothing could be more pitifully descriptive of the tragedy of John Keats than his sonnet to Fanny Brawne. Here, in its expression of unconsummated love, is an agonized outcry. The young poet's uncontrollable and jealousy-ridden passion is voiced in an utterance that stammers its way through tantalizing memories of the beloved's "minor zest of love, your kiss" and her "warm, white, lucent, million-pleasured breast." It breaks out in a wild demand—"O! let me have thee whole,—all—all—be mine!" and affects us all the more poignantly because we know that the intensity of his emotion was heightened by the fevered tuberculosis which killed Keats at twenty-six.

HEINRICH HEINE (1797–1856) Two things are remarkable about this poem by Heinrich Heine. Instead of the colloquial lyrics for which he is famous, it is a classical sonnet, a form he seldom employed; unlike his bittersweet and often cynical songs in the *Buch der Lieder,* it is a tender and almost reverential tribute to his mother. Heine's worldly sophistication and his sense of persecution were forgotten when the proud, suffering son wrote these humble fourteen lines.

ELIZABETH BARRETT BROWNING (1806–1861) It was with a hope of renewed life that the invalid Elizabeth Barrett secretly married and ran off with the young poet Robert Browning, six years her junior. And it was with profound gratitude that she presented him with the series reflecting courtship and marriage entitled *Sonnets from the Portuguese.* The title was both a disguise and a playful intimacy. The poems were not translations and the title was a wifely reminder to her husband who, because of her olive complexion, teasingly called her "my little Portuguese."

DANTE GABRIEL ROSSETTI (1828-1882) Son of an Italian poet and political refugee, Dante Gabriel Rossetti became the leader of a group which called itself the Pre-Raphaelite Brotherhood, indicating that they believed arts and letters had declined after the advent of Raphael. A painter as well as a poet, Rossetti's verse excels in sensuous and graphic effects.

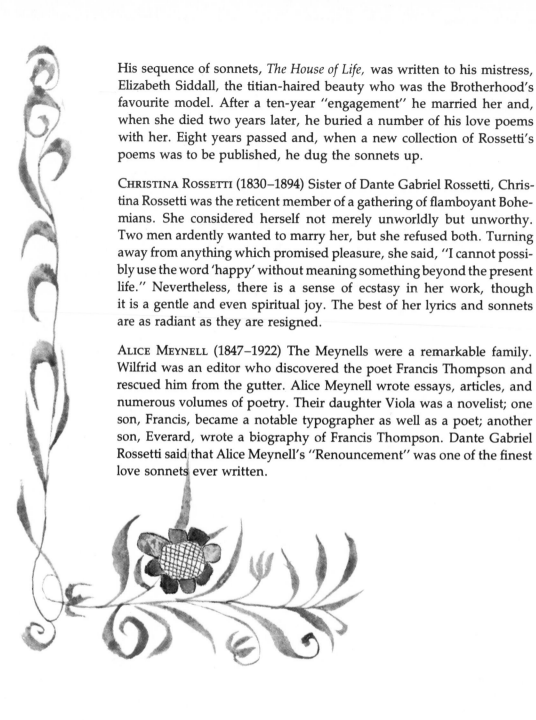

His sequence of sonnets, *The House of Life,* was written to his mistress, Elizabeth Siddall, the titian-haired beauty who was the Brotherhood's favourite model. After a ten-year "engagement" he married her and, when she died two years later, he buried a number of his love poems with her. Eight years passed and, when a new collection of Rossetti's poems was to be published, he dug the sonnets up.

CHRISTINA ROSSETTI (1830–1894) Sister of Dante Gabriel Rossetti, Christina Rossetti was the reticent member of a gathering of flamboyant Bohemians. She considered herself not merely unworldly but unworthy. Two men ardently wanted to marry her, but she refused both. Turning away from anything which promised pleasure, she said, "I cannot possibly use the word 'happy' without meaning something beyond the present life." Nevertheless, there is a sense of ecstasy in her work, though it is a gentle and even spiritual joy. The best of her lyrics and sonnets are as radiant as they are resigned.

ALICE MEYNELL (1847–1922) The Meynells were a remarkable family. Wilfrid was an editor who discovered the poet Francis Thompson and rescued him from the gutter. Alice Meynell wrote essays, articles, and numerous volumes of poetry. Their daughter Viola was a novelist; one son, Francis, became a notable typographer as well as a poet; another son, Everard, wrote a biography of Francis Thompson. Dante Gabriel Rossetti said that Alice Meynell's "Renouncement" was one of the finest love sonnets ever written.